The differences in laws and practices result in radically different patterns of employment and hours *adjustments* to cyclical and structural changes in Europe than in the U.S. European producers adjust employment levels much less and more slowly, relying more on adjustments through hours measures (or preventive), than U.S. producers.

Report of the U.S. Secretary of Labor's Task Force on Economic Adjustment and Worker Dislocation

1 Introduction

Many analysts of the effects of income protection and job protection policies utilize comparisons between West European and U.S. labor demand behavior.[1] Such analysts, from both sides of the Atlantic, assert that North American employers vary employment to a greater degree and average hours per worker to a lesser degree than West European firms in response to changes in desired labor inputs (because of changes in real labor costs, real materials and energy prices, etc.). I have not documented the views of North American and European policymakers on comparative labor demand propositions. I suspect however that the conventional wisdom among scholarly analysts of such policies likely holds sway in larger policy circles.

What is the empirical evidence on North American versus West European employment and hours adjustment? Several investigators find that West European employers adjust employment to a lesser extent than U.S. employers.[2] This result stems from comparison of simple standard deviations of aggregate manufacturing employment for the U.S. and one or more West European

---

[1] Recent examples include:

1. Burtless's [4] discussion of the empirical evidence supporting the Baily–Feldstein hypothesis that enhanced experience-rating of unemployment insurance finance increases layoff costs and lowers the incidence of layoffs.

2. Burdett and Wright's [3] investigation of the implications of a short-time compensation unemployment scheme versus restricting unemployment insurance to laid-off workers.

3. Fitzroy and Hart's [6] examination of the implications of a quasi-fixed payroll tax to finance UI versus a variable payroll tax.

4. Abraham and Houseman's [1] investigation of the impact of statutory severance payments to laid-off workers on labor market flexibility.

[2] E.g. Bertola [2], Tachibanaki [30], and Gordon [9].

1

countries. Recent studies that focus on the estimation of a dynamic labor demand model find that manufacturing employment adjustment in West Europe resembles that in North America. These studies employ divergent methodologies and examine different countries.

Symons and Layard [28] estimate the standard adjustment cost model of dynamic labor demand. Their estimated speed of employment adjustment parameter for France equals that for Canada and exceeds that for America. Abraham and Houseman [1] examine the production worker employment elasticity with respect to output among disaggregate manufacturing industries. They find that in most industries the West German 12-month and 18-month employment elasticities equal or exceed the American. The West German and American 1-month employment elasticities tend not to be significantly different. Finally, Mairesse and Dormont [17] uniquely employ micro level panel data to estimate the elasticity of employment growth with respect to product demand growth among French, West German, and American manufacturing firms. They do not find that the U.S. estimated elasticity is significantly higher than West Germany's, though it is significantly higher than France's. They conclude that "Despite the diversity of situations and evolutions of French, German, and US manufacturing over the period 1970-79, the labor and investment demand behaviors of large firms in the three countries are in fact largely comparable. This is the main message of the analysis..."

This paper carefully examines the speed of employment and average hours per worker adjustment among manufacturing industries in North America and Great Britain. The empirical equations estimated derive from the adjustment cost model of dynamic labor demand. The speed of adjustment parameters reflect the size of the nonrecurring labor costs borne by the firm, i.e. hiring and firing costs. Furthermore, the behavior of the demand for operatives (as opposed to all types of workers) among disaggregate manufacturing industries is examined in order to better avoid well-known aggregation biases complicating the analysis of labor demand adjustment of total employment in the aggregate manufacturing sector.

This study finds that British manufacturing industries do not possess a lower speed of employment adjustment and a higher speed of average hours per worker adjustment than North American industries, with the exception of the vehicles industry. This finding is consistent with the hypothesis that the nonrecurring labor costs borne by these industrial firms are similar in size in Great Britain and North America. The empirical results also indicate that industries characterized by a relatively high speed of employment adjustment possess a relatively high

2

speed of average hours adjustment. This contradicts the frequent assertion that labor input adjustment occurs along the employment or hours per worker margin, but not both. Intuitively, firms that rapidly bring actual employment close to desired employment can rapidly return actual hours per worker to its desired level.

Ancillary to the primary motivation of the paper, the econometric analysis of the determinants of labor demand reveals that the real wage rate appears to influence short-run labor demand tenuously at best. In assessing the role of the real wage rate, I find not surprisingly that most of the real wage rate series appear to be integrated. Since all the British operative employment series reject the unit root hypothesis, the data indicate that, among the industries examined, the real wage rate does not influence British operative employment. An analogous analysis suggests that the real wage rate impacts average hours worked in few of the manufacturing industries in any of three countries considered.

The paper proceeds as follows. Section 2 presents a cursory treatment of the adjustment cost model of dynamic labor demand. Section 3 examines the static solution to the firm's labor input optimization. It presents the comparative statics in regard to hours per worker and some intuition for the form of the dynamic decision rule. Readers familiar with the adjustment cost model may elect to skip it. Section 4 reviews Sargent's [25] method of treating the firm's expectations of future magnitudes in the dynamic employment equation. Section 5 outlines the data and presents some descriptive statistics. Section 6 highlights the econometric procedures performed and how I report the econometric results. It summarizes the integration properties of the time series and elaborates on the consequences of the presence of unit roots on the reporting of the econometric results. Section 7 discusses the econometric results. Section 8 draws conclusions.

2　The Adjustment Cost Model of Dynamic Labor Demand

The adjustment cost model of dynamic labor demand traces its origins at least back to Holt *et al* [14]. It is quite analogous to the capital stock adjustment models of the Lucas [16] and Gould [10] vintage. As the model is the staple of the dynamic labor demand literature only an abbreviated treatment is provided.[3] The version I present derives from Wickens'[33] discrete time model.

The firm chooses its employment level $N(t)$ and hours per worker $H(t)$ to maximize prof-

---

[3] See Nickell's [18] seminal survey for extensions and details.

its. The firm experiences nonrecurring labor costs that are a quadratic function of net new hires. Wage costs are described by the convex earnings-hours locus $W(H(t))$. Hence the firm's multiperiod optimization problem is:

$$\underset{N(t), H(t)}{\text{MAX}} \sum_{t=0}^{\infty} R^t \left\{ p(t)Q\left(N(t), H(t)\right) - [W\left(H(t)\right) + f(t)]N(t) - \frac{a_2}{2}\left[N(t) - N(t-1) + s(t)\right]^2 \right\} \tag{1}$$

where:

$R \equiv$ discount factor,

$p(t) \equiv$ exogenous product price,

$Q\left(N(t), H(t)\right) \equiv$ production function with the usual derivative properties,

$f(t) \equiv$ recurring quasi-fixed labor costs (e.g. group insurance plan contributions) per worker,

$a_2 \equiv$ adjustment cost parameter,

$s(t) \equiv$ voluntary separations.

Upon differentiation, first-order expansion of the first-order conditions, and evaluation of a second-order difference equation, one derives the fundamental employment and hours equations:

$$N(t) = \lambda_N N(t-1) + (1 - \lambda_N)\left[(1 - \lambda_N R)\sum_{s=0}^{\infty}\lambda_N^s R^s E_t\left[N^*(t+s)\right]\right] \tag{2}$$

$$H(t) = \lambda_H H(t-1) + (1 - \lambda_H)\left[(1 - \lambda_H R)\sum_{s=0}^{\infty}\lambda_H^s R^s E_t\left[H^*(t+s)\right]\right] \tag{3}$$

where:

$(1 - \lambda_i) \equiv$ "the speed of adjustment parameter" , i= N, H ,

$E_t[\cdot] \equiv$ conditional expectations operator,

$N^*(t), H^*(t) \equiv$ "desired employment, desired average hours per worker" or employment and average hours per worker in the absence of adjustment costs.

Equations (2) and (3) are simple partial adjustment mechanisms. The firm sets employment and average hours per worker between yesterday's level and their long-run targets, the long-run targets being a geometrically weighted average of all expected future and current desired levels. Hence the speed of employment adjustment parameter, for example, $(1 - \lambda_N)$, is the fraction of the discrepancy between yesterday's employment and target employment the firm makes up today. It can be shown that it depends inversely on the size of the firm's nonrecurring labor costs per worker.

3 Employment and Hours in the Static Solution

Readers unfamiliar with the adjustment cost model of dynamic labor demand may benefit from a brief discussion of the static solution to the maximization of equation (1) above. This will serve two purposes. First, in section 7 of the paper I present empirical results on the impact of the real wage rate on employment and average hours per worker. What signs should we expect? In this section I will derive the comparative statics. Second, an understanding of the static solution assists in comprehending the further complexities of the dynamic solution.

Maximization of equation (1) generates first order conditions:

$$R^t \left[p(t)Q_N - (W(H(t)) + f(t)) - a_2 (N(t) - N(t-1) + s(t)) \right] \tag{4}$$

$$+ R^{t+1} a_2 (N(t+1) - N(t) + s(t+1)) = 0$$

$$R^t (p(t)Q_H - W_H N(t)) = 0. \tag{5}$$

Suppose the firm could at no cost adjust the size of its work force, i.e. nonrecurring labor costs equal zero or $a_2 = 0$. Denote the employment and hours per worker fulfilling the first order conditions again "desired employment" and "desired average hours per worker" or $N^*(t)$ and $H^*(t)$. Equations (4) and (5) may be rewritten:

$$Q_N = \frac{W(H^*(t)) + f(t)}{p(t)} \tag{6}$$

$$W_H = \frac{Q_H H^*(t)}{Q_N N^*(t)} \cdot \frac{W(H^*(t)) + f(t)}{H^*(t)}. \tag{7}$$

Equation (6) is the familiar equality of the marginal physical product of labor to the real labor costs per worker. From it we anticipate that an increase in the real labor costs per worker lowers desired employment. Equation (7) indicates that at the optimum the marginal hourly labor cost will be proportional to the average hourly labor cost.

In order to make progress on the static determination of average hours per worker and perform interesting comparative statics, follow Wickens [33] and assume a simple form of the earnings-hours locus:

$$W(H(t)) = \begin{cases} w_B H(t) & \text{if } H(t) < H_B \\ w_B H_B + b w_B (H(t) - H_B) & \text{otherwise} \end{cases}$$

where w_B is the straighttime wage rate, H_B=normal hours, and $(b-1)$ is the overtime premium.

Consider initially equation (7) if $\frac{Q_H H^*(t)}{Q_N N^*(t)}$ exceeded unity. This condition then requires that the marginal hourly labor cost exceed the average hourly labor cost. This can not be fulfilled if $H^*(t) < H_B$ as $W_H = w_B$ is below $\overline{W} = w_B + \frac{f(t)}{H(t)}$. Alternatively if $H^*(t) > H_B$ then the marginal hourly labor cost could exceed the average as $W_H = bw_B$ and $\overline{W} = bw_B + \frac{f(t)-(b-1)H_B w_B}{H^*(t)}$. If $f(t) - (b-1)H_B w_B < 0$ then the marginal hourly labor cost exceeds the average hourly labor cost. This does *not* imply however that when $\frac{Q_H H^*(t)}{Q_N N^*(t)} > 1$ then $H^*(t) > H_B$ is a profit maximizing equilibrium. The necessary condition is fulfilled but the firm can do better. Note that $\overline{W} = bw_B + \frac{f(t)-(b-1)H_B w_B}{H^*(t)}$ rises as $H^*(t)$ rises if $f(t)-(b-1)H_B w_B < 0$. Thus the firm can clearly lower its labor cost per worker by cutting back hours to H_B. Hours per worker fall and average hourly labor costs fall if $H^*(t) = H_B$. So when $\frac{Q_H H^*(t)}{Q_N N^*(t)} > 1$, $H^*(t) = H_B$ is the only profit maximizing equilibrium (and only if $f(t) - (b-1)H_B w_B < 0$).

The hours outcome is less determinate if $\frac{Q_H H^*(t)}{Q_N N^*(t)} < 1$. In this instance the necessary condition dictates that the average hourly labor cost exceed the marginal. This is clearly fulfilled if $H^*(t) < H_B$. Suppose that $f(t) - (b-1)H_B w_B > 0$. Then the condition may also be fulfilled if $H^*(t) > H_B$. If $H^*(t) > H_B$ then $W_H = bw_B$ and $\overline{W} = bw_B + \frac{f(t)+(b-1)H_B w_B}{H^*(t)} > W_H$. Thus we see that when $\frac{Q_H H^*(t)}{Q_N N^*(t)} < 1$ the equilibrium hours per worker need not be unique and scheduled overtime might be a static equilibrium.

The comparative statics of changes in the parameters of the earnings–hours locus, w_B, b, and $f(t)$, can be derived in fairly straightforward fashion. It goes without saying that if $H^*(t) = H_B$

these partial derivatives might be zero. When $H^*(t) \neq H_B$ then[4]

$$\frac{\partial H^*(t)}{\partial w_B} < 0 \; , \qquad \frac{\partial H^*(t)}{\partial b} \leq 0 \; , \qquad \frac{\partial H^*(t)}{\partial f(t)} > 0$$

Permit me to proceed to the pursuit of the second purpose of this section. What is the intuition for equations (2) and (3)? Suppose adjustment costs are zero, i.e. the firm can costlessly hire and fire as many workers as it wishes. If in the current period the real wage rate increases, profit maximization dictates that the firm instantaneously alter employment and hours per worker to their desired levels, regardless of the size of the adjustment. Would the firm ever need to form expectations of the future? No, because whatever changes the future holds the firm can immediately and costlessly alter the labor inputs at the future date. In the absence of adjustment costs, the firm need not form expectations of future levels of the work force and hours per worker.[5]

If it is costly to alter the size of the work force, then the firm may find it profitable to have its actual employment level and actual hours per worker level depart from the static optimum ($N^*(t)$ and $H^*(t)$). Departures of $N(t)$ and $H(t)$ from $N^*(t)$ and $H^*(t)$ must entail a sacrifice of profits (in the absence of adjustment costs). But getting to $N^*(t)$ and $H^*(t)$ entail adjustment

---

[4]When $H^*(t) \neq H_B$ then it must be the case that $\frac{Q_H H^*(t)}{Q_N N^*(t)} < 1$ from the analysis in the text. The following comparative statics are derived under the easiest case that $\frac{\partial \frac{Q_H H^*(t)}{Q_N N^*(t)}}{\partial H(t)} = 0$. Suppose $H^*(t) < H_B$. Then partial differentiation of $H^*(t)$ yields:

$$\frac{\partial H^*(t)}{\partial w_B} = \frac{Q_H H^*(t)}{Q_N N^*(t) - Q_H H^*(t)} \cdot \frac{-f(t)}{w_B^2} < 0$$

$$\frac{\partial H^*(t)}{\partial f(t)} = \frac{Q_H H^*(t)}{Q_N N^*(t) - Q_H H^*(t)} \cdot \frac{1}{w_B} > 0$$

Alternatively suppose that $H^*(t) > H_B$. Then

$$H^*(t) = \frac{Q_H H^*(t)}{Q_N N^*(t)} \cdot \frac{W(H^*(t)) + f(t)}{W_H} = \frac{Q_H H^*(t)}{Q_N N^*(t)} \cdot \frac{w_B H_B + b w_B (H^*(t) - H_B) + f(t)}{b w_B}$$

Here:

$$\frac{\partial H^*(t)}{\partial w_B} = \frac{Q_H H^*(t)}{Q_N N^*(t) - Q_H H^*(t)} \cdot \frac{-f(t)}{b w_B^2} < 0$$

$$\frac{\partial H^*(t)}{\partial b} = \frac{Q_H H^*(t)}{Q_N N^*(t) - Q_H H^*(t)} \cdot \frac{-(w_B H_B + f(t))}{b^2 w_B} < 0$$

$$\frac{\partial H^*(t)}{\partial f(t)} = \frac{Q_H H^*(t)}{Q_N N^*(t) - Q_H H^*(t)} \cdot \frac{1}{b w_B} > 0$$

---

[5]This point was originally made by Kennan [15].

7

costs and these added costs may outweigh the gain of the static profits. The profit maximizing solution under quadratic adjustment costs is partial adjustment. The firm moves part of the way toward $N^*(t)$ and $H^*(t)$. How far? To the point at which the added adjustment costs just offset the gain of static profit from further movement.

In regard to equation (3), the discussion earlier in this section indicated that generally $H^*(t) \neq H_B$. Since I have assumed explicitly that there are no costs of adjusting hours per worker, why would $H(t)$ ever depart from $H^*(t)$? It is profitable for the firm to have actual hours depart from desired hours when actual employment is away from desired employment. As the firm returns actual employment to its target level, it returns actual hours to its target level. Since employment follows a partial adjustment mechanism, so does hours per worker.

4   Modelling the Firm's Expectations of the Future Forcing Variables

In order to make equations (2) and (3) empirically operational we must model the firm's expectations of future desired employment levels and desired average hours per worker. In the case of employment, suppose desired employment linearly depends on the $(n \times 1)$ column vector of exogenous variables $Z(t)$:

$$N^*(t) = h'_N Z(t) + \varepsilon_1(t) \tag{8}$$

where h'_N is a vector of parameters expressing the desired relationship between $N(t)$ and $Z(t)$ and $\varepsilon_1(t) \sim \mathrm{N}(0, \sigma^2)$.

Since the focus of the empirical work is on the estimation of the speeds of employment and hours adjustment, and not the most accurate expectational models, I follow Sargent [25] and model the exogenous variables $Z(t)$ as univariate autoregressive time series processes[6]:

$$
\begin{bmatrix}
A_1(L) & 0 & \cdots & 0 \\
0 & A_2(L) & \cdots & 0 \\
\vdots & \vdots & \vdots & \vdots \\
0 & 0 & 0 & A_n(L)
\end{bmatrix}
Z(t) = v(t) \tag{9}
$$

where $A_i(L)$ is a lag operator polynomial and $v(t)$ is a vector of white noise disturbances. Substitution of equation (8) and the expectation of (9) into equation (2) generates the conven-

---

[6]See Nickell [19] for an example of an empirical dynamic labor demand model that treats expectations more carefully.

tional empirical employment equation[7]:

$$N(t) = \lambda_N N(t-1) + B(L)'Z(t) + U_1(t) \tag{10}$$

where $U_1(t)$ is distributed $U_1(t) \sim \mathrm{N}(0, \sigma^2)$ and $B(L)'$ is a vector of lag operator polynomials:

$$B(L)' = [B_1(L) \ \ B_2(L) \ \ \dots \ \ B_n(L)]$$

Note that the order of the lag operator polynomial for each exogenous variable need not be equal. The orders deemed appropriate for the autoregressive time series models in equation (9) dictate the orders of the lag operator polynomials $B_1(L)$, $B_2(L)$, $\dots$, $B_n(L)$.[8]

Sargent's procedure may also be used in identical fashion to implement the fundamental hours equation (3). Thus the empirical work focuses on estimation of equation (10) and:

$$H(t) = \lambda_H H(t-1) + C(L)'Z(t) + U_2(t) \tag{11}$$

5   Data and Descriptive Statistics

Well-known aggregation arguments suggest that the lag structure of equations (2) and (3) is highly simplistic. In particular Nickell [18] shows that aggregation of different types of labor (with presumably different adjustment costs) will generate multiple lags of the dependent variable on the right-hand side. For this reason this study does not use aggregate employment and average hours per worker but operative employment and average hours worked per operative.

Monthly data on operative employment and hours worked per operative for Great Britain are available for the four manufacturing groups shown in Table 1 as well as the aggregate manufacturing sector. Similar series can be constructed for Canada and the U.S.[9] The industrial composition of the four manufacturing groups accord fairly closely across the three countries, the exception being that the North American vehicles groups (group 2) include the ship and

---

[7]Convergence of the infinite sum in equation (2) requires that the autoregressive time series models in equation (9) fulfill certain technical assumptions. See Sargent [25] for details.

[8]I.e., if lag order p_i appears most appropriate for the autoregressive time series model of $Z_i(t)$, then $(p_i - 1)$ lags of $Z_i(t)$ appear in equation (6).

[9]Published monthly observations for British operatives' employment and weekly hours worked per operative are unavailable after 1980. Canada substantially revised its establishment survey at 1983 and hence comparable series for employment, hours, and wage rates are unavailable prior to 1983.3.

boat building and repairing industries while Britain's order XI does not. Appendix table 7 indicates the relative size of the manufacturing groups in terms of employment.

In regard to exogenous variables, a real wage rate measure and a measure of quantity demand exist for the manufacturing groups on a monthly basis. Appendix tables 8 and 9 display the variable definitions and data sources. Single country studies often include a measure of real materials and energy prices, the capital stock, and quasi-fixed recurring labor costs. Measures of such variables do not exist on a disaggregated basis and are omitted herein. All the data are seasonally unadjusted.

Table 2 shows the volatility of the raw series. The time series have not been detrended; nor have any seasonal cycles been eliminated, etc. Depicted are the standard deviations of the monthly percentage change, i.e.:

$$\sqrt{\mathrm{Var}\left(\frac{x(t) - x(t-1)}{x(t-1)} \times 100\right)}$$

For both aggregate manufacturing and the disaggregate manufacturing industries, operative employment and average hours worked per operative do not conform to the conventional wisdom. British manufacturing industries display the largest volatility of operative employment. Among the disaggregate manufacturing groups Canada displays the greatest variation in average hours worked per operative. These statistics do not control for the volatility of the determinants of the labor demand variables. The simplest check might be to simply tabulate the ratio of the standard deviations of operative employment and average hours worked per operative to the standard deviation of the measure of quantity demand. Table 3 displays these ratios. Little is claimed for these simple statistics except that hopefully they pique the readers' interest in a more sophisticated analysis of employment and hours adjustment.[10]

6   Econometric Procedures

The results reported in this section utilize the natural logarithm of all time series. This specification conforms to prior single country dynamic labor demand studies. Tables 4 and 5 examine the integration properties of the univariate time series using simple Dickey–Fuller [5] unit root tests. Tables 4 and 5 indicate that the Dickey–Fuller test rejects the unit root hypothesis for all average hours worked per operative series and most of the quantity demand

---

[10]The British employment data, for example, exhibit a significant amount of summer season variation. The standard deviation of the monthly employment growth rates deleting the July, August, and September observations are 0.77, 1.28, 0.88, 0.92, and 0.57 .

10

series. Several of the North American employment series fail to reject the unit root hypothesis as do many of the British and U.S. real wage rate series.

The fully efficient estimation technique estimates the operative employment or average hours worked per operative model and the expectational models of equation (5) jointly using FIML. However, on grounds of practicality, the need to estimate 30 separate employment and hours models precluded using simultaneous equation estimation techniques. Instead, single equation estimation techniques were used. Nickell's [19] empirical results on the United Kingdom's aggregate manufacturing employment suggest single equation estimation techniques generate similar parameter estimates to FIML's.

Estimation of the univariate autoregressive expectational models in equation (5) proceeded in simple fashion. Arbitrarily it was assumed that the highest possible order of autoregression is two.[11] The time series analysis then proceeded using a Box–Jenkins model selection strategy. The robustness of the estimated employment and hours equations to relaxation of the AR order restriction will be commented on below.

The employment and hours models included a constant and a linear *trend* to proxy the missing capital stock. Inclusion of seasonal dummies substantially increased $\overline{R}^2$.

Autocorrelated error disturbances can have particularly serious implications in the presence of a lagged dependent variable. If the dependent variable is stationary, then autocorrelated disturbances generate not only inconsistent estimates of the standard errors of the least squares estimators but also inconsistent estimators of the coefficients.[12] If however the dependent variable is integrated, OLS estimators of the coefficients need not be inconsistent. Phillips [21] shows this in a model lacking a time trend and wherein the dependent variable has no drift. West [32] extends the consistency property to an integrated variable with drift (but again no time trend). Sims, Stock, and Watson [26] show that consistent coefficient estimates generally obtain in the presence of a deterministic time trend and variables with arbitrary orders of integration. They assume classical disturbances however.

---

[11]This simplification can be motivated by examination of past researchers' experience. Generally, time series analysts advise that most economic time series can be adequately modelled as low-order processes (see e.g. Pyndyck and Rubinfeld [22] p. 532 and Granger [11] p. 65). Specifically, Rosanna [23] found that a random walk worked as well as any other univariate time series specification for modelling real wages and new orders for six two-digit U.S. manufacturing industries.

[12]See e.g. Pyndyck and Rubinfeld [22] p. 193.

Since inconsistent coefficient estimates need not obtain when the regression disturbance is autocorrelated, the following reporting procedures are followed. If Durbin's h *test* or m *test* rejects the null hypothesis of zero first-order autocorrelation (at the 5% level) and the dependent variable appears stationary, then I report the results of the equation estimated via the maximum likelihood autocorrelation correction procedure. Otherwise OLS estimation results are reported.

Appendix tables 10 to 15 report the estimated operative employment and average hours worked per operative equations.[13] These tables omit the results on the coefficients on the trend, seasonals, and the constant. Note that not all t-ratios are reported. In instances the t-ratio will not possess its usual asymptotic normal distribution and its value is unreported. This occurs (a) when the dependent variable appears integrated[14] or (b) the regressor appears integrated (in the anomalous situation of a dependent variable whose Dickey–Fuller test rejected the unit root hypothesis). Table 6 records the estimated speeds of employment and hours adjustment utilizing the low-order equations.

The specification of the employment and hours equations reported in appendix tables 10 to 15 involves two important assumptions.

First, the specification imposes on the data the single lagged dependent variable structure of equations (2) and (3) without testing. This course might be rationalized by reference to Nickell's empirical findings on the United Kingdom:

> Operatives form a large, homogeneous group of manual workers making up some
> 75% of total employment and in the corresponding operatives employment function
> there is definitely only one lag on employment. (Nickell [19]).

Second, the estimation of the autoregressive expectational models of equation (5) assumes the highest possible order of autoregression is two. In order to explore the importance of this

---

[13]The U.S. employment model of the vehicles industry is particularly sensitive to the inclusion of a couple of sample observations. During October and November 1970 production worker employment precipitously fell under 1 million workers (to 970 thousand). It averaged 1.25 million workers over the sample and these are the only observations possessing less than 1 million workers. Interestingly however the index of industrial production for the vehicles industry also reached its minimum at 1970.10 and 1970.11. The estimated speed of employment adjustment using the full sample is 1.03, whereas with these observations excluded it falls to 0.36. Because the latter estimate is much closer to that obtained using subsamples of the full sample period, appendix table 12 and table 6 report the results of the restricted sample's equation.

[14]Stock and West [27] indicate that only t-tests on *mean zero* stationary regressors (or that can be written as such) have an asymptotic normal distribution in this instance.

restriction for the estimation of the employment and hours models the highest possible lag of the independent variables is identified for each of the 15 observational units. This can be determined by examination of the independent variables' partial autocorrelation function. Then each employment and hours model is estimated using all lag lengths between the low-order and highest possible lag length.[15] The minimum AIC model is identified and compared to the AIC value of the low-order model. For all the British and U.S. models the difference between AIC values is at most 1.0 . Among the Canadian models eight equations have a difference of AIC values above 1.0 but never exceed 3.8 . Hence on the basis of the AIC restricting attention to a low-order of autoregression is justified.[16]

7 Econometric Results

Previous dynamic labor demand studies find that simple employment functions fit the data quite well. Appendix tables 10 to 12 reveal that this is also true for our disaggregate manufacturing industries. Perusal of appendix tables 13 to 15 indicates that the simple hours models estimated are not successful. The goodness of fit tends to be low and the estimated speeds of hours adjustment possess large estimated standard errors.[17] The most obvious explanation of these impotent hours results is simply that I have omitted key variables in the determination of hours per worker. However, Rosanna's [24,23] work focuses on the determinants of average hours worked and includes additional explanatory variables beyond those I use in this study. His equations do not possess much more explanatory power than those reported in appendix table 15.

Across countries the Canadian equations have the greatest difficulty explaining the variation

---

[15] The real wage rate and quantity demand measure were constrained to possessing the same lag length.

[16] Note that the more common approach to testing the lag structure on the independent variables is to determine an upper bound order of a short order lag polynomial and then to judge if lower order models are appropriate by successively dropping the longest lag if the t-ratios meet certain criterion. See for example Symons [29] and Symons and Layard [28]. The deletion of longer lags on these grounds will be unwarranted in some circumstances. For example, as described above, if the right-hand side includes a deterministic time trend and the dependent variable is integrated, typically the regressors will not have an asymptotic normal distribution.

[17] Hazeldine's [13] study also examined both employment and average hours worked among disaggregate manufacturing industries in the United Kingdom. His estimated hours equations tend to fit better than the corresponding employment equations. Among Rosanna's [23] six U.S. two-digit manufacturing industries the $\overline{R}^2$ of the employment equation exceeds that of the average hours worked equation.

of operative employment and average hours worked per operative. This might be due to the smaller Canadian sample size. Furthermore, the construction of the Canadian quantity demand measure, real shipments, involved deflating. Hence, the absence of perfectly disaggregated wholesale price data affects the quantity demand variable in addition to the real wage rate measure.

Though the results on average hours worked per operative should be treated with caution, one may conclude on the basis of table 6 that:

1. Examining disaggregate manufacturing industries, there is not evidence that British employers adjust operative employment to a lesser extent and average hours worked per operative to a greater extent than North American employers, controlling for the determinants of these inputs. The vehicles industry is the only industry whose estimated speeds of employment and hours adjustment conform to the conventional characterization that West Europe adjusts along the intensive margin, not the extensive margin, in comparison to the U.S.[18]

The integration properties of the time series do make it difficult to know the precision of the estimates. The result that adjustment appears similar, with the exception of vehicles, does not rely however on the absence of statistically significant differences. The estimated British speeds are simply not the expected relative size in comparison to the North American speeds.[19]

What of the result that the estimated speeds of the aggregate manufacturing sector spin a different story?[20] This discrepancy is interesting and an aspect for further research.

---

[18] The sample for the U.S. extends into the 1980's, whereas the British data only span the 1970's. The bottom half of table 6 indicates that this result remains unaltered if identical sample lengths are utilized.

[19] Note, however, that I am uncertain that all of the OLS estimates are consistent. As alluded to in section 6, regression with an integrated dependent variable and with a deterministic time trend yields consistent estimators assuming classical disturbances. As far as I know, no one has proved consistency of the estimators in this instance allowing for autocorrelated error disturbances.

[20] All the results reported for Great Britain utilize the "average earnings index: all employees (old series)" as the nominal wage rate measure. The employment and hours variables apply only to operatives. Furthermore this wage rate measure is inappropriate since it indexes weekly earnings, not the straighttime hourly wage rate. On this basis and the poor empirical performance of the average earnings index an alternative nominal wage measure was tried. A monthly "index of the basic hourly wage rate" of manual workers is available during

However, at this juncture it can be recalled that there exist *a priori* grounds for preferring the impression derived from examining less aggregated data:

(a) Obviously the industrial composition of the aggregate manufacturing sector may differ across countries.

(b) Aggregation of equations (2) and (3) over firms can corrupt the single lagged dependent variable specification presumed herein. Nickell's work quoted earlier indicates this is not a problem for the United Kingdom's aggregate manufacturing sector. It might be for the North American aggregate manufacturing sectors. Simply put, the logic of the complexities arising from aggregation over firms dictates a preference for the less aggregated results.

2. In all countries there exists a *positive* correlation between the estimated speeds of employment and hours adjustment. Within each country the industries characterized by high employment adjustment possess high hours adjustment. Topel's [31] employment and hours models for seven two-digit U.S. manufacturing industries also display this feature

the 1970's for the nondurable manufacturing groups and aggregate manufacturing. Note that it applies to the United Kingdom, not Great Britain. It performed similarly to the average earnings index, the exception being the aggregate manufacturing equations. The estimated employment and hours models are:

$$(1 - 0.8870\ L)N(t) = (0.0618 + 0.0032\ L)Q(t) - 0.0240\ RBHW(t) + e(t)$$
$$(25.046) \qquad (3.6149) \qquad (0.1840)$$

$$N{=}120 \quad \overline{R}^2 = 0.9960 \quad \text{Durbin's h}{=}0.8436$$

$$(1 - 0.4831\ L)H(t) = (0.1983 - 0.0916\ L)Q(t) - 0.0486\ RBHW(t) + e(t)$$
$$(5.7389) \qquad (4.9906) \qquad (-2.1617)$$

$$N{=}120 \quad \overline{R}^2 = 0.6303 \quad \text{Durbin's h}{=}{-}1.7359$$

The employment outcome focuses attention on the imprecise estimation of the speed of adjustment parameter. It is disconcerting that altering real wage rate measures changes the estimated adjustment speed by 50%. However the estimates of $(1 - \lambda_N)$ with real average earnings on the right-hand side versus the real basic hourly wage rate are not significantly different from one another. We simply are not obtaining narrow estimates of the adjustment speed.

(though he did not emphasize this result).[21] Of the manufacturing industries examined in this project, vehicles and textiles tend to be the high employment and hours adjustment industries in each country.

The empirical analysis also sheds some light on the role of the real wage rate in empirical dynamic labor demand models. Previous empirical studies have not routinely found real wage rates to possess either large elasticities or statistically significant coefficients. Wrong-signed real wage rates coefficients have been estimated.[22] This paper's contribution to this investigation are four-fold.

First, strong evidence shows that the importance of real wage rates can not be assessed by simple hypothesis testing (t-tests and F tests and Wald tests). This derives from the observation that the monthly real wage rate series often appear integrated. In table 5 almost all the British and U.S. real wage rate series fail to reject the unit root hypothesis. Suppose real wage rates are integrated and a deterministic time trend is included in the employment function (as is common practice). Then generally the real wage rate coefficients do not have an asymptotic normal distribution and standard inference is invalid. The implication is simply that assessing the real wage rate's statistical significance requires investigation of its integration properties. Thus, for example, Symons' [29] finding that the real wage rate terms significantly impact total employment in the British aggregate manufacturing sector *may* be invalid.

Second, the monthly data do not indicate that the real wage rate influences operative employment in Great Britain. This judgement arises from consideration of the following simple linear time series model of West [32]:

$$\mathrm{w}(t) = \alpha + \gamma \mathrm{y}(t) + \mathrm{e}(t)$$

α and γ are scalars to be estimated and $\mathrm{e}(t)$ is a stationary regression disturbance. Let $\mathrm{y}(t)$ be integrated. Then either $\gamma \neq 0$ and $\mathrm{w}(t)$ is integrated or $\gamma = 0$ and $\mathrm{w}(t)$ is stationary. Tables 4 and 5 show that most of the British real wage rate series appear integrated but none

---

[21]This is not so apparent in his estimated speeds of adjustment (Table 5) but very visible in his estimated employment and hours impact elasticities with respect to current forecasted demand and unforeseen demand innovations (Table 6).

[22]See e.g. Nickell and Symons [20], Symons and Layard [28], and Hazeldine's [12] discussions of the role of real labor costs in dynamic employment equations.

of the British operative employment series accept the unit root hypothesis. Hence, for British operative employment, the industries examined do not seem to indicate a role for the real wage rate. Furthermore, this simple sort of evidence would not be reversed if real materials and energy prices and other omitted variables were available.

Third, the integration properties of the average hours worked per operative series also do not indicate a pervasive role for the real wage rate in any of the countries. Table 4 shows that none of the average hours worked per operative series appear integrated. In the eleven instances in which the real wage rate series accepts the unit root hypothesis then it appears real wage rates do not influence employers choice of average hours worked.

Fourth, theoretically one expects the elasticity of average hours worked per operative with respect to the real wage rate to be negative. Many of the British and U.S. real wage rate elasticities embedded in the real wage rate coefficients reported in appendix tables 14 and 15 possess positive signs. This finding however may result from the omission of relevant explanatory variables. Rosanna [23] reports a negative relationship for four of six two-digit U.S. manufacturing industries.

Finally, I conclude this section with an explicit note on estimation procedures for dynamic labor demand equations. Since Nickell [19] it has been recognized that imposing the simple lag structure of equations (2) or (3) on the data is unwise without testing. If, however, the employment or average hours series is integrated, the "empiricist approach" to specifying the labor demand equation faces formidable difficulties. In this instance inclusion of a deterministic time trend generally results in the OLS estimators being not asymptotically normal. Hence, the specification search requires a foray into nonconventional hypothesis testing. Barring that route, at least two alternatives exist. One could rely on theory to dictate the specification (a bitter pill to swallow though it may be). Alternatively, one could rely on less aggregated data (the route I opted for).

8 Conclusion

This study finds that among disaggregate manufacturing industries, Britain does not possess lower speeds of employment adjustment and higher speeds of hours adjustment than the U.S., with the exception of the vehicles industry. Rather the estimated speeds are similar. This finding complements the results of several recent comparative dynamic labor demand investigations (reviewed in the introduction). Together this body of research challenges the prevalent

17

notion among labor market policy analysts that West European employers differ in their labor utilization choices in response to product demand and real labor cost shocks in comparison to U.S. firms.

It should perhaps be stressed that a finding of similar adjustment speeds need not imply similar elasticities of actual employment and actual average hours worked with respect to the forcing variables. Rather the adjustment cost model of dynamic labor demand generates a partial adjustment type of decision rule. The "adjustment speed" refers to the tendency to alter the actual labor demand variable in response to movements of the desired labor demand variable. This parameter is of particular interest since it reflects the size of the nonrecurring labor costs borne by the firm. Hence, in theory adjustment speeds have a tighter connection to the costs imposed on the firm due to job security policies than the elasticity of the actual labor demand variable with respect to a forcing variable (which Abraham and Houseman [1] and Mairesse and Dormont [17] estimate).

A finding of similar adjustment speeds between West Europe and the U.S. is consistent with several alternative hypotheses regarding the impact of income and job protection policies on employers. One alternative (which analysts of such policies are not prone to believe) is simply that such policies' bark is worse than their bite. In other words, the aggregate costs these policies impose on the firm is simply not of a sufficient magnitude to observably alter the firm's adjustment behavior. Alternatively, these policies may impact employers' behavior and the aggregate costs imposed at the margin on employers are similar across countries. For example, in the context of Great Britain and the U.S., the British employer's cost at the margin due to the statutory severance payment to a redundant worker (on average) approximates an average U.S. employer's cost (at the margin) for a redundant worker's unemployment insurance benefits (via experience-rating of unemployment insurance finance).[23] Other alternative explanations exist but such a finding is not consistent with the existence of a sizable difference in nonrecurring labor costs across these countries.

The study's result that industries that possess relatively high employment adjustment speeds also possess relatively high hours adjustment speeds is easily understood in the context of the adjustment cost model of the firm sketched in section 2. In Wickens' [33] model, by assumption, there do not exist costs of adjusting hours per worker. Actual hours only depart from steady-

---

[23]See e.g. Fry [7].

state hours because actual employment deviates from steady-state employment. Hence the quicker the firm returns actual employment to steady-state employment, the quicker actual hours return to steady-state hours. In the absence of costs of hours adjustment, the model predicts that firms that rapidly adjust employment also rapidly adjust hours.

Table 1: Composition of the Four Major Manufacturing Groups

1968 SIC Code	Manufacturing Industry

1. Engineering, allied industries (except vehicles)

order VII	Mechanical engineering
order VIII	Instrument engineering
order IX	Electrical engineering
order X	Shipbuilding and marine engineering
order XII	Metal goods, n.e.s.

2. Vehicles

order XI	Vehicles and other transport equipment

3. Textiles, leather, and clothing

order XIII	Textiles
order XIV	Leather, leather goods, and fur
order XV	Clothing and footwear

4. Food, drink, and tobacco

order III	Food, drink, and tobacco

Table 2: Standard Deviation of Monthly Percentage Changes (in %)

| | Standard Deviation | | |
var/major manufac. group	Great Britain	Canada	U.S.
Operative Employment			
Engineering	8.21	2.32	1.14
Vehicles	6.41	2.23	3.88
Textiles	9.20	3.09	1.99
Food	4.84	4.86	3.08
All manufac.	7.84	2.12	1.24
Average Hours Worked per Operative			
Engineering	1.83	1.96	1.47
Vehicles	2.69	3.81	2.52
Textiles	2.35	3.17	2.19
Food	0.836	1.45	1.10
All manufac.	1.62	1.57	1.32
Real wage rate			
Engineering	2.10	0.89	0.587
Vehicles	2.84	1.33	1.26
Textiles	1.92	1.92	1.20
Food	3.39	1.68	1.36
All manufac.	1.71	0.774	0.854
Nominal wage rate			
Engineering	2.12	0.708	0.419
Vehicles	2.76	1.12	0.908
Textiles	1.93	1.93	0.579
Food	3.22	1.52	0.775
All manufac.	1.59	0.712	0.533
Quantity demand			
Engineering	9.18	8.89	2.11
Vehicles	9.74	16.1	6.65
Textiles	10.0	11.1	7.55
Food	6.15	6.26	7.77
All manufac.	8.04	6.72	2.94

For all series other than the quantity demand measure the sample is:

Great Britain: 1970.1 – 1980.12

Canada: 1983.3 – 1988.12

U.S.: 1970.1 – 1988.12

For the quantity demand series the sample lengths are:

Great Britain: 1970.1 – 1980.3

Canada: 1983.3 – 1987.9

U.S.: 1970.1 – 1988.12

Table 3: Ratios of the Standard Deviation of the Employment Change and the Hours Change to the Standard Deviation of the Quantity Demand Change

major manufac. group	employment			hours		
	Great Britain	Canada	U.S.	Great Britain	Canada	U.S.
Engineering	0.89	0.26	0.54	0.20	0.22	0.70
Vehicles	0.66	0.14	0.58	0.28	0.23	0.38
Textiles	0.92	0.28	0.26	0.24	0.29	0.29
Food	0.79	0.78	0.40	0.14	0.23	0.14
All manufac.	0.98	0.32	0.42	0.20	0.23	0.45

Table 4: Unit Root Statistics

$$x(t) = \hat{\mu} + \hat{\rho}x(t-1) + e(t)$$

Country/Statistic	Log Levels of Series				
	Engineering	Vehicles	Textiles	Food	All manufac.

Operative Employment

Canada

T	69	69	69	69	69
$\hat{\tau}_\mu(x(t))$	-1.00	-1.76	-3.29*	-2.36	-1.59
$\hat{t}(\mu_{x(t)})$	1.02	1.80	3.29	2.26	1.60
$\hat{\tau}_\mu(\Delta x(t))$	-8.45**	-7.37**		-4.57**	-5.46**
$\hat{t}(\mu_{\Delta x(t)})$	0.78	1.31		-0.06	0.35

Great Britain

T	129	129	129	129	129
$\hat{\tau}_\mu(x(t))$	-5.53**	-4.77**	-3.25*	-5.16**	-4.93**
$\hat{t}(\mu_{x(t)})$	5.53	4.76	3.23	5.16	4.92

U.S.

T	227	224	227	227	227
$\hat{\tau}_\mu(x(t))$	-1.17	-3.24*	-1.16	-4.17**	-1.73
$\hat{t}(\mu_{x(t)})$	1.16	3.24	1.14	4.17	1.73
$\hat{\tau}_\mu(\Delta x(t))$	-10.85**		-20.80**		-13.53**
$\hat{t}(\mu_{\Delta x(t)})$	-0.25		-1.62		-0.32

Average Hours Worked per Operative

Canada

T	69	69	69	69	69
$\hat{\tau}_\mu(x(t))$	-6.29**	-6.54**	-7.82**	-5.17**	-7.79**
$\hat{t}(\mu_{x(t)})$	6.29	6.54	7.82	5.17	7.79

Great Britain

T	129	129	129	129	129
$\hat{\tau}_\mu(x(t))$	-3.97**	-4.43**	-4.80**	-3.99**	-4.07**
$\hat{t}(\mu_{x(t)})$	3.97	4.42	4.79	3.99	4.07

U.S.

T	227	227	227	227	227
$\hat{\tau}_\mu(x(t))$	-6.48**	-7.36**	-6.82**	-6.09**	-6.07**
$\hat{t}(\mu_{x(t)})$	6.48	7.36	6.82	6.09	6.07

Sample: Great Britain: 1970.1 – 1980.12
Canada: 1983.3 – 1988.12
U.S.: 1970.1 – 1988.12

Notes: T $\equiv$ number of observations. Significant at the **1% , *5% , and †10% level. $\hat{\tau}_\mu(x(t))$ denotes the Dickey–Fuller [5] t-statistic for the univariate series $x(t)$. Critical values are from Fuller [8] p. 373. $\hat{t}(\mu)$ is the ratio of the OLS estimate of the constant to its estimated standard error. $\hat{t}(\mu)$ is not asymptotically normally distributed.

Table 5: Unit Root Statistics (cont.)

$$x(t) = \hat{\mu} + \hat{\rho}x(t-1) + e(t)$$

Country/Statistic	Log Levels of Series				
	Engineering	Vehicles	Textiles	Food	All manufac.
Quantity Demand					
Canada					
T	54	54	54	54	54
$\hat{\tau}_\mu(x(t))$	-3.47*	-4.49**	-4.49**	-5.57**	-3.91**
$\hat{t}(\mu_{x(t)})$	3.47	4.49	4.50	5.58	3.91
Great Britain					
T	122	122	122	122	122
$\hat{\tau}_\mu(x(t))$	-7.43**	-6.04**	-7.79**	-5.55**	-7.40**
$\hat{t}(\mu_{x(t)})$	7.43	6.03	7.79	5.56	7.40
U.S.					
T	227	224	227	227	227
$\hat{\tau}_\mu(x(t))$	-0.98	-2.43	-6.86**	-5.99**	-1.21
$\hat{t}(\mu_{x(t)})$	1.06	2.45	6.85	6.00	1.27
$\hat{\tau}_\mu(\Delta x(t))$	-14.92**	-14.27**			-15.24**
$\hat{t}(\mu_{\Delta x(t)})$	1.82	0.47			1.35
Real Wage Rate					
Canada					
T	69	69	69	69	69
$\hat{\tau}_\mu(x(t))$	-3.36*	-2.18	-4.02**	-2.70†	-1.89
$\hat{t}(\mu_{x(t)})$	3.36	2.17	4.02	2.70	1.90
$\hat{\tau}_\mu(\Delta x(t))$		-8.40**			-9.33**
$\hat{t}(\mu_{\Delta x(t)})$		-0.24			0.80
Great Britain					
T	126	126	129	129	126
$\hat{\tau}_\mu(x(t))$	-1.80	-1.80	-1.83	-3.05*	-2.45
$\hat{t}(\mu_{x(t)})$	1.81	1.79	1.85	3.06	2.46
$\hat{\tau}_\mu(\Delta x(t))$	-14.53**	-12.20**	-13.15**		-10.95**
$\hat{t}(\mu_{\Delta x(t)})$	1.01	-0.27	1.72		0.60
U.S.					
T	227	227	227	227	227
$\hat{\tau}_\mu(x(t))$	-0.94	-2.21	-1.62	-1.70	-1.17
$\hat{t}(\mu_{x(t)})$	0.96	2.22	1.59	1.69	1.17
$\hat{\tau}_\mu(\Delta x(t))$	-14.34**	-17.54**	-13.33**	-11.97**	-15.36**
$\hat{t}(\mu_{\Delta x(t)})$	0.58	0.72	-0.56	-0.21	0.36

Notes: T ≡ number of observations. Significant at the **1% , *5% , and †10% level. $\hat{\tau}_\mu(x(t))$ denotes the Dickey-Fuller [5] t-statistic for the univariate series $x(t)$. Critical values are from Fuller [8] p. 373. $\hat{t}(\mu)$ is the ratio of the OLS estimate of the constant to its estimated standard error. $\hat{t}(\mu)$ is not asymptotically normally distributed.

Table 6: Speeds of Employment and Hours Adjustment Estimated on the basis of the Low-order Models[‡]

	employment			hours		
	Great Britain	Canada	U.S.	Great Britain	Canada	U.S.
Engineering	0.11	0.07	0.10	0.32	0.48	0.51
	(0.04)			(0.07)	(0.16)	(0.06)
Vehicles	0.11	0.37	0.36	0.88°	0.86	0.60
	(0.05)		(0.03)	(0.15)	(0.15)	(0.06)
Textiles	0.17	0.28	0.11	1.00°	1.14°	0.24°
	(0.06)	(0.13)		(0.07)	(0.08)	(0.05)
Food	0.10	0.12	0.09	0.14°	0.70	0.19°
	(0.04)		(0.03)	(0.05)	(0.15)	(0.04)
All manufac	0.07	0.08	0.25	0.96°	0.82	1.32°
	(0.03)			(0.11)	(0.14)	(0.06)

Sample:Great Britain: 1970.1 – 1980.3
      Canada: 1983.3 – 1987.9
      U.S.: 1970.1 – 1988.12

Estimated standard errors in parentheses
Parameter estimates that do not have a standard error reported do not have an asymptotic normal distribution.
°Estimated from the MLE of ρ autocorrelation correction equation.

[‡]U.S. Speeds of Employment and Hours Adjustment Estimated on the basis of 1970.1 – 1980.3

Engineering	0.09	1.26°
		(0.10)
Vehicles	0.36	0.65
	(0.05)	(0.09)
Textiles	0.14	1.16°
		(0.11)
Food	0.08	0.46
	(0.04)	(0.08)
All manufac	0.30	0.65
		(0.09)

Estimated standard errors in parentheses
Parameter estimates that do not have a standard error reported do not have an asymptotic normal distribution.
°Estimated from the MLE of ρ autocorrelation correction equation.

APPENDIX

Table 7: Size (in 1000's) and Share of Employment (in %)

| | | Country | | |
		Great Britain[†]	Canada	U.S.
	T	60	70	228
	Average Employment Level	2477.3	242.41	4299.6
Engineering	Average Share of Manufacturing Employment	35.3	20.8	31.3
	Average Employment Level	740.17	137.57	1248.5
Vehicles	Average Share of Manufacturing Employment	10.5	11.8	9.1
	Average Employment Level	850.87	129.00	2011.4
Textiles	Average Share of Manufacturing Employment	12.1	11.1	14.6
	Average Employment Level	684.45	157.97	1211.7
Food	Average Share of Manufacturing Employment	9.7	13.6	8.8
All manufacturing	Average Employment Level	7027.3	1163.8	13722.
	Average Share of Total Employment	n.a.[°]	12.6*	14.8**

Sample: Great Britain: 1976.1 – 1980.12
   Canada: 1983.3 – 1988.12
   U.S.: 1970.1 – 1988.12

T ≡ number of observations.

[†]British operative employment is an index so this table uses British total employees in employment. Hence the absolute employment levels for Great Britain are not comparable to the North American.

[°]The Department of Employment does not publish a monthly employees in employment figure for all industries. Using the quarterly figures, economywide employment averaged 22.117 million over the sample period, resulting in a manufacturing share of about 31.8%.

* $\frac{\text{total employees paid by the hour in manufacturing}}{\text{total employment in industrial aggregate (1970 SIC 031-951)}}$

** $\frac{\text{total production worker employment in manufacturing}}{\text{total employment (not just production workers) on nonagricultural payrolls}}$

Table 8: Variable Definitions of Data for Great Britain and the U.S.

GREAT BRITAIN
1970.1 – 1980.12

hours: "index of average weekly hours worked per operative" seasonally unadjusted actual hours worked   Source: *Dept. of Employment Gazette* and *British Labour Statistics Yearbook 1976*

employment: operative employment seasonally unadjusted   this is not a published variable but constructed from other published series

$$= \frac{\text{index of total weekly hours worked by all operatives}}{\text{index of average weekly hours worked per operative}}$$

Source: *Dept. of Employment Gazette* and *British Labour Statistics Yearbook 1976*

wage rate: "average earnings index: all employees: by industry (old series)" seasonally unadjusted   total renumeration received in the form of money, including bonuses, excluding employers' contributions to national insurance and pension funds   Source: *Dept. of Employment Gazette* and *British Labour Statistics Yearbook 1976*

quantity demand: "index of industrial production " seasonally unadjusted   Source: *Monthly Digest of Statistics*

output price: "index number of wholesale prices" seasonally unadjusted   Source: *Monthly Digest of Statistics*

U.S.
1970.1 – 1988.12

hours: "average weekly hours of production workers" seasonally unadjusted   hours paid for, including hours of paid absence (holidays, vacation, and sick leave) Source: BLS *Employment, Hours, and Earnings–National* Data tape

employment: "employment of production workers" seasonally unadjusted   Source: BLS *Employment, Hours, and Earnings–National* Data tape

wage rate: "average hourly earnings, excluding overtime, of production workers" seasonally unadjusted   total money renumeration, excluding irregularly paid bonuses and employers' contributions to pension funds and social security and other insurance programs   does not include overtime paid at time and a half but does not adjust for other premium pay provisions, such as holiday pay and late-shift work   Source: BLS *Employment, Hours, and Earnings–National* Data tape

quantity demand: Federal Reserve Board's "index of industrial production" seasonally unadjusted   Source: *Industrial Production*

output price: "producer price index" seasonally unadjusted   Source: BLS *Producer Price Indexes*

Table 9: Variable Definitions of Data for Canada

CANADA

1983.3 – 1988.12

hours: "average weekly hours of employees paid by the hour" seasonally unadjusted hours paid for, including hours of paid absence Source: *Employment, earnings and hours*

employment: "number of employees paid by the hour" seasonally unadjusted Source: *Employment, earnings and hours*

wage rate: average hourly earnings, excluding overtime, of employees paid by the hour seasonally unadjusted this is not a published variable but constructed from other published series

$$= \frac{\text{avg. weekly earnings (excluding overtime)}}{\text{avg. weekly hours} - \text{avg. weekly overtime hours}}$$

the definition of earnings mirrors the U.S. defintion of earnings Source: *Employment, earnings and hours*

quantity demand: "value of shipments" seasonally unadjusted in nominal terms and needs to be deflated Source: *Canadian Statistical Review*

output price: "industrial product price index, by industry" seasonally unadjusted Source: *Industry Price Indexes*

Table 10: Low-order Canadian OLS Employment Equations

Sample: 1983.3 – 1987.9

	Engineering	Vehicles	Textiles	Food	All manufac.
$N(t-1)$	0.9289	0.6340	0.7243	0.8767	0.9186
			(5.7802)		
$Q(t)$	-0.0616	0.0211	0.0123	-0.0820	-0.1291
			(0.0918)		
$Q(t-1)$			-0.0125		
			(-0.0946)		
$RW(t)$	0.1104	0.0433	-0.1420	-0.2489	-0.1067
			(-0.6930)		
$RW(t-1)$				-0.0185	
T	54	54	54	54	54
$\bar{R}^2$	0.8876	0.9282	0.7218	0.9658	0.9425
F	28.90	46.67	9.59	94.65	58.89
s	0.0198	0.0187	0.0232	0.0172	0.0130
Durbin's h	1.4280	9.7602	-1.9389	-0.5815	2.6159
AIC	-7.6	-7.7	-7.3	-7.9	-7.9

$N(t) \equiv$ log operative employment.

$Q(t) \equiv$ log quantity demand.

$RW(t) \equiv$ log real wage rate.

T $\equiv$ number of observations.

t-ratios in parentheses.

Coefficient estimates that do not have a t-ratio reported do not have an asymptotic normal distribution.

s=standard error of the regression.

Table 11: Low-order British OLS Employment Equations

Sample 1970.1 – 1980.3

	Engineering	Vehicles	Textiles	Food	All manufac.
$N(t-1)$	0.8875	0.8895	0.8305	0.9001	0.9293
	(20.280)	(18.206)	(14.357)	(25.270)	(32.653)
$Q(t)$	0.0442	0.0463	0.0617	0.0701	0.0412
	(1.4114)	(2.0325)	(2.7129)	(3.2633)	(2.2789)
$Q(t-1)$	0.0197	-0.0215	0.0048		0.0007
	(0.6351)	(-1.0429)	(0.2231)		(0.0369)
$RW(t)$	0.0000	0.0087	-0.0541	-0.0084	-0.0005
				(-0.2785)	
$RW(t-1)$	-0.0002			-0.0022	
				(-0.0727)	
T	115	117	119	118	117
$\bar{R}^2$	0.9881	0.9672	0.9963	0.9838	0.9956
F	558.01	214.55	2011.6	444.99	1648.1
s	0.0085	0.0130	0.0077	0.0067	0.0052
Durbin's h	-0.6274	-1.7264	1.2806	0.5048	- 1.3264
AIC	-9.4	-8.6	-9.6	-9.9	-10.4

$N(t) \equiv$ log operative employment.

$Q(t) \equiv$ log quantity demand.

$RW(t) \equiv$ log real wage rate.

$T \equiv$ number of observations.

t-ratios in parentheses.

Coefficient estimates that do not have a t-ratio reported do not have an asymptotic normal distribution.

s=standard error of the regression.

Table 12: Low-order U.S. OLS Employment Equations

Sample: 1970.1 – 1988.12

	Engineering	Vehicles	Textiles	Food	All manufac.
$N(t-1)$	0.8979	0.6426	0.8909	0.9113	0.7458
		(20.262)		(30.767)	
$Q(t)$	0.1194	0.2406	0.1536	0.0084	0.2342
				(0.4036)	
$Q(t-1)$			-0.0662	-0.0188	
				(-0.8874)	
$RW(t)$	-0.0205	-0.2760	0.0109	-0.0798	-0.0948
$RW(t-1)$				0.0927	
T	227	224	227	227	227
$\bar{R}^2$	0.9896	0.9469	0.9967	0.9784	0.9889
F	1429	266.04	4307	603.83	1349
s	0.0075	0.0171	0.0071	0.0084	0.0061
Durbin's h	8.3678	-0.2231	4.9356	1.0944	7.0778
AIC	-9.6	-8.3	-9.8	-9.5	-10.3

$N(t) \equiv$ log operative employment.

$Q(t) \equiv$ log quantity demand.

$RW(t) \equiv$ log real wage rate.

T $\equiv$ number of observations.

t-ratios in parentheses.

Coefficient estimates that do not have a t-ratio reported do not have an asymptotic normal distribution.

s=standard error of the regression.

Table 13: Low-order Canadian Hours Equations

Sample: 1983.3 – 1987.9

	Engineering	Vehicles	Textiles°	Food	All manufac.
$H(t-1)$	0.5191	0.1441	-0.1397	0.2958	0.1830
	(3.2915)	(0.9566)	(-1.6985)	(1.9941)	(1.3050)
$Q(t)$	0.0404	0.1047	-0.0250	0.1848	0.0875
	(0.9706)	(2.6397)	(-0.3831)	(2.5726)	(2.9284)
$Q(t-1)$			-0.0497		
			(-0.7813)		
$RW(t)$	-0.0733	0.1441	-1.0353	-0.2408	-0.0523
	(-0.6703)		(-10.205)	(-1.5823)	
$RW(t-1)$				0.1298	
				(0.8353)	
T	54	54	54	54	54
$\bar{R}^2$	0.8211	0.3054	0.6794	0.6254	0.7908
F	17.22	2.55		6.53	14.35
s	0.0072	0.0248	0.0119	0.0083	0.0052
Durbin's h	‡	‡		‡	‡
AIC	-9.6	-7.2	-8.2	-9.3	-10.3

$H(t) \equiv$ log average hours per operative.

$Q(t) \equiv$ log quantity demand.

$RW(t) \equiv$ log real wage rate.

T $\equiv$ number of observations.

t-ratios in parentheses.

Coefficient estimates that do not have a t-ratio reported do not have an asymptotic normal distribution.

s=standard error of the regression.

°Estimated from the MLE of ρ autocorrelation correction equation.

‡Durbin's h test could not be computed. Durbin's m test could not reject the null hypothesis of zero first-order autocorrelation (at the 5% level at maximum).

Table 14: Low-order British Hours Equations

Sample: 1970.1 – 1980.3

	Engineering	Vehicles°	Textiles°	Food°	All manufac.°
$H(t-1)$	0.6771	0.1226	-0.0046	0.8630	0.0408
	(9.1521)	(0.8313)	(-0.0634)	(18.072)	(0.3796)
$Q(t)$	0.1002	0.1122	0.1448	0.0226	0.1159
	(2.2789)	(3.5260)	(3.8504)	(1.8955)	(3.4043)
$Q(t-1)$	-0.0698	0.0398	0.1211		0.0694
	(-1.5965)	(1.2649)	(3.0975)		(1.8928)
$RW(t)$	0.0033	-0.0075	0.5625	0.0126	0.0011
				(0.7618)	
$RW(t-1)$	-0.0032			-0.0155	
				(-0.9274)	
T	115	117	119	118	117
$\bar{R}^2$	0.6734	0.4087	0.7077	0.8823	0.6929
F	14.828				
s	0.0123	0.0181	0.0125	0.0038	0.0098
Durbin's h	0.3744				
AIC	-8.6	-7.7	-8.5	-10.9	-9.0

$H(t) \equiv$ log average hours per operative.

$Q(t) \equiv$ log quantity demand.

$RW(t) \equiv$ log real wage rate.

T $\equiv$ number of observations.

t-ratios in parentheses.

Coefficient estimates that do not have a t-ratio reported do not have an asymptotic normal distribution.

s=standard error of the regression.

°Estimated from the MLE of ρ autocorrelation correction equation.

Table 15: Low-order U.S. Hours Equations

Sample: 1970.1 – 1988.12

	Engineering	Vehicles	Textiles°	Food°	All manufac.°
$H(t-1)$	0.4946	0.4003	0.7645	0.8088	-0.3205
	(8.5980)	(6.6921)	(16.072)	(19.264)	(-4.9903)
$Q(t)$	0.0779	0.0691	0.1836	0.0266	0.2351
			(4.7955)	(1.8115)	
$Q(t-1)$			-0.1589	-0.0059	
			(-4.1753)	(-0.3917)	
$RW(t)$	0.1238	0.1180	0.0423	-0.0610	0.0583
$RW(t-1)$				0.0751	
T	227	227	227	227	227
$\bar{R}^2$	0.8065	0.7010	0.6685	0.8264	0.8271
F	63.79	36.33			
s	0.0080	0.0157	0.0146	0.0058	0.0069
Durbin's h	-1.2732	-1.5591			
AIC	-9.4	-8.2	-8.1	-10.1	-9.7

$H(t) \equiv$ log average hours per operative.

$Q(t) \equiv$ log quantity demand.

$RW(t) \equiv$ log real wage rate.

$T \equiv$ number of observations.

t-ratios in parentheses.

Coefficient estimates that do not have a t-ratio reported do not have an asymptotic normal distribution.

s=standard error of the regression.

°Estimated from the MLE of ρ autocorrection equation.

References

[1] Katherine G. Abraham and Susan N. Houseman. Employment and hours adjustment: a U.S./German comparison. April 1988.

[2] Giuseppe Bertola. Job security, employment, and wages. *European Economic Review*, 34:851–79, June 1990.

[3] Kenneth Burdett and Randall Wright. Unemployment insurance and short-time compensation: the effects on layoffs, hours per worker, and wages. *Journal of Political Economy*, 97:1479–96, December 1989.

[4] Gary Burtless. Jobless pay and high European unemployment. In Robert Z. Lawrence and Charles T. Schultze, editors, *Barriers to European Growth: A Transatlantic View*, Brookings, Washington, D.C., 1987.

[5] David A. Dickey and Wayne A. Fuller. Distribution of the estimators for autoregressive time series with a unit root. *Journal of the American Statistical Association*, 74:427–31, June 1979.

[6] Felix R. Fitzroy and Robert A. Hart. Hours, layoffs and unemployment insurance funding: theory and practice in an international perspective. *The Economic Journal*, 95:700–13, Supplement 1985.

[7] Richard A. Fry. Unemployment insurance and international employment and hours adjustment. September 1990. Unpublished Ph.D. thesis essay.

[8] Wayne A. Fuller. *Introduction to Statistical Time Series*. John Wiley, New York, 1976.

[9] Robert J. Gordon. Why U.S. wage and employment behavior differs from that in Britain and Japan. *The Economic Journal*, 92:13–44, March 1982.

[10] J. Gould. Adjustment costs in the theory of investment of the firm. *Review of Economic Studies*, 35:47–55, 1968.

[11] C. W. J. Granger. *Forecasting in Business and Economics*. Academic Press, New York, 1980.

[12] Tim Hazeldine. 'Employment functions' and the demand for labour in the short-run. In Zmira Hornstein, Joseph Grice, and Alfred Webb, editors, *The Economics of the Labour Market*, HMSO, London, 1981.

[13] Tim Hazeldine. New specifications for employment and hours functions. *Economica*, 45:179–93, May 1978.

[14] C. C. Holt et al. *Planning Production, Inventories, and Work Force*. Prentice-Hall, Englewood Cliffs, N.J., 1960.

[15] John Kennan. The estimation of partial adjustment models with rational expectations. *Econometrica*, 1441–56, 1979.

[16] R. Lucas. Optimal investment policy and the flexible accelerator. *International Economic Review*, 8:78–85, 1967.

[17] Jacques Mairesse and Brigette Dormont. Labor and investment demand at the firm level: a comparison of French, German, and U.S. manufacturing, 1970-79. February 1985. NBER Working Paper #1554.

[18] Stephen Nickell. Dynamic models of labour demand. In O. Ashenfelter and R. Layard, editors, *Handbook of Labour Economics*, Elsevier, 1986.

[19] Stephen Nickell. An investigation of the determinants of manufacturing employment in the United Kingdom. *Review of Economic Studies*, 51:529–57, October 1984.

[20] Stephen Nickell and James Symons. The real wage–employment relationship in the United States. *Journal of Labor Economics*, 8:1–15, 1990.

[21] P. C. B. Phillips. Time series regression with a unit root. *Econometrica*, 55:277–301, March 1987.

[22] Robert S. Pyndyck and Daniel S. Rubinfeld. *Econometric Models and Economic Forecasts*. McGraw-Hill, New York, second edition, 1981.

[23] Robert J. Rosanna. Buffer stocks and labor demand: further evidence. *Review of Economics and Statistics*, 67:16–26, February 1985.

[24] Robert J. Rosanna. Some empirical estimates of the demand for hours in U.S. manufacturing industries. *Review of Economics and Statistics*, 65:560–9, November 1983.

[25] T. J. Sargent. Estimation of dynamic labor demand schedules under rational expectations. *Journal of Political Economy*, 86:1009–45, 1978.

[26] Christopher A. Sims, James H. Stock, and Mark W. Watson. Inference in linear time series models with some unit roots. February 1987. Hoover Institution Working Papers in Economics E-87-1.

[27] James H. Stock and Kenneth D. West. Integrated regressors and tests of the permanent-income hypothesis. *Journal of Monetary Economics*, 21:85–95, January 1988.

[28] J. Symons and R. Layard. Neoclassical demand for labour functions for six major economies. *The Economic Journal*, 94:788–98, December 1984.

[29] J. S. V. Symons. Relative prices and the demand for labour in British manufacturing. *Economica*, 52:37–49, 1985.

[30] Toshiaki Tachibanaki. Labour market flexibility in Japan in comparison with Europe and the U.S. *European Economic Review*, 31:647–84, April 1987.

[31] Robert H. Topel. Inventories, layoffs, and the short-run demand for labor. *American Economic Review*, 72:769–87, September 1982.

[32] Kenneth D. West. Asymptotic normality when regressors have a unit root. March 1986. Princeton University Discussion Papers in Economics #110.

[33] M. R. Wickens. Towards a theory of the labour market. *Economica*, 41:278–94, August 1974.

www.ingramcontent.com/pod-product-compliance
Lightning Source LLC
Chambersburg PA
CBHW081312180526
45170CB00007B/2669